A New Indian Comic Opera in two acts. Entitled the Nautch Girl: or, the Rajah of Chutneypore. Libretto by George Dance. Music by Edward Solomon. With lyrics by George Dance and Frank Desprez.

George Dance, Frank Desprez

A New Indian Comic Opera in two acts. Entitled the Nautch Girl: or, the Rajah of Chutneypore.
Libretto by George Dance. Music by Edward Solomon. With lyrics by George Dance and Frank
Desprez.
Dance, George
British Library, Historical Print Editions
British Library
Desprez, Frank
1891].
48 p. ; 8°.
11779.g.7.(5.)

The BiblioLife Network

This project was made possible in part by the BiblioLife Network (BLN), a project aimed at addressing some of the huge challenges facing book preservationists around the world. The BLN includes libraries, library networks, archives, subject matter experts, online communities and library service providers. We believe every book ever published should be available as a high-quality print reproduction; printed on- demand anywhere in the world. This insures the ongoing accessibility of the content and helps generate sustainable revenue for the libraries and organizations that work to preserve these important materials.

The following book is in the "public domain" and represents an authentic reproduction of the text as printed by the original publisher. While we have attempted to accurately maintain the integrity of the original work, there are sometimes problems with the original book or micro-film from which the books were digitized. This can result in minor errors in reproduction. Possible imperfections include missing and blurred pages, poor pictures, markings and other reproduction issues beyond our control. Because this work is culturally important, we have made it available as part of our commitment to protecting, preserving, and promoting the world's literature.

GUIDE TO FOLD-OUTS, MAPS and OVERSIZED IMAGES

In an online database, page images do not need to conform to the size restrictions found in a printed book. When converting these images back into a printed bound book, the page sizes are standardized in ways that maintain the detail of the original. For large images, such as fold-out maps, the original page image is split into two or more pages.

Guidelines used to determine the split of oversize pages:

• Some images are split vertically; large images require vertical and horizontal splits.
• For horizontal splits, the content is split left to right.
• For vertical splits, the content is split from top to bottom.
• For both vertical and horizontal splits, the image is processed from top left to bottom right.

A New Indian Comic Opera,

IN TWO ACTS,

ENTITLED

THE NAUTCH GIRL

OR,

The Rajah of Chutneypore.

Libretto by

GEORGE DANCE

Music by

EDWARD SOLOMON

With Lyrics by

GEORGE DANCE & FRANK DESPREZ.

———→●◆●←———

London:

CHAPPELL & CO., 50, NEW BOND STREET, W.

———

PRICE ONE SHILLING.

A New Indian Comic Opera.

IN TWO ACTS.

ENTITLED

THE NAUTCH GIRL;

OR,

THE RAJAH OF CHUTNEYPORE.

LIBRETTO BY
GEORGE DANCE.

MUSIC BY
EDWARD SOLOMON.

WITH LYRICS BY
GEORGE DANCE AND FRANK DESPREZ.

PRICE ONE SHILLING.

London:

CHAPPELL & CO., 50, NEW BOND STREET, W.

FIRST PRODUCED AT THE SAVOY THEATRE, LONDON, BY
MR. R. D'OYLY CARTE, ON TUESDAY, 30TH JUNE, 1891.

Dramatis Personœ.

PUNKA (*The Rajah of Chutneypore*)	...MR. RUTLAND BARRINGTON.
INDRU (*His Son*)	... MR. COURTICE POUNDS.
PYJAMA (*The Grand Vizier*) ...	... MR. FRANK THORNTON.

CHINNA LOOFA		MISS JESSIE BOND.
SUTTEE	(*Punka's Poor Relations*)	MISS SAUMAREZ.
CHEETAH		MISS LAWRENCE.

BABOO CURRIE (*Proprietor of a Nautch Troupe*)	MR. FRANK WYATT.

HOLLEE BEEBEE		MISS LENORE SNYDER.
BANYAN	(*Nautch Girls*)	MISS LOUIE ROWE.
KALEE		MISS ANNIE COLE.
TIFFIN		MISS CORA TINNIE.

BUMBO (*An Idol*)	MR. W. H. DENNY.

Nautch Girls, Ladies of the Court, Soldiers, Priests, Coolies, &c.

ACT I.
A STREET IN THE OUTSKIRTS OF CHUTNEYPORE ... *Mr. T. E. Ryan.*

ACT II.
COURTYARD OF THE RAJAH'S PALACE ... ... *Mr. J. Harker.*

The Opera produced under the Stage Direction of Mr. CHARLES HARRIS, and the Musical Direction of Mr. FRANÇOIS CELLIER, assisted by Mr. ERNEST FORD. The Dances arranged by Mr. JOHN D'AUBAN. The Costumes designed by Mr. PERCY ANDERSON and executed by Miss FISHER, Mdmes. AUGUSTE and M. ALIAS. Wigs by CLARKSON. Properties by Mr. SKELLY. Stage Machinist, Mr. SHELDON.

THE NAUTCH GIRL;

OR,

THE RAJAH OF CHUTNEYPORE.

ACT I.

(A street in the outskirts of Chutneypore, SUDRAS discovered.)

OPENING CHORUS.

Beneath the sky of blue
The indolent Hindu
    Reclines the whole day long.
He scorns all worldly trouble,
For life's a fragile bubble,
    And death a sweet, sweet song.
He scorns ambitious schemes,
He weaves no lofty dreams,
    His glance is on the ground.
Why tinge to-day with sorrow
When with the dark to-morrow
    Grim Siva's call may sound?

Enter INDRU.

RECITATIVE.—INDRU.

This is the place, the sweet and hallowed spot,
And these the folks who share her humble lot.

SUDRAS *(salaaming)*. Salaam, Sahib! Salaam, Sahib!

ARIA.—INDRU.

Bow not, good people, to the earth,
We are all men of equal worth;
For though a Brahmin such as I
By Hindu law may not come nigh
Plebeian fellows such as ye,
Yet I despise that harsh decree.
The year, the day, the hour is past
When men should serve the despot Caste.
    So, there's a hand, and there's a hand,
    And grasp it firm and true!
    I love you much, for I am such
    A democrat Hindu.

CHORUS.   Yes, there's a hand, &c.
These sentiments are democrat indeed,
But who is this that preaches such a creed?

INDRU. I am Indru, the Rajah's only son.

CHORUS. He is Indru, the Rajah's only son.

        (*They fall back salaaming.*)

RECITATIVE.—INDRU.

Nay, shrink not from me. Rank I have eschewed.
I am your brother, from this day henceforth;
I love a maid, one of your humble caste,
'Mongst you she lives, and where *she* lives, live I;
You are her friends, and Beebee's friends are mine.
List and I'll tell the story of our love.

BALLAD.—INDRU.

The sun was setting, cool the day,
And, half asleep, I dreaming lay.
When, through the window from the street,
There came a voice so clear and sweet.
  'Twas like the surf o'er pebbles tripping
  Or drops of water drip, drip, dripping
   In a crystal stream.
 'Twas not an ordinary voice
  But something like a dream.

CHORUS.   'Twas not, &c.

I rose, and to the casement flew,
And what a vision met my view!
A dancing maid, a thing of grace,
A Nautch girl with an angel's face.
  'Twas like a cherub's calmly sleeping,
  Or Venus through her tresses peeping
   At her bashful love.
 'Twas not an ordinary face,
  But something from above.

CHORUS.   'Twas not, &c.

    Enter BABOO CURRIE.

CURRIE. Who sings of love in such flowery accents?

INDRU. Baboo Currie! (CURRIE *salaams.*) Won't you shake
hands?

CURRIE. Not with the Rajah's son.

INDRU. Why not?

CURRIE. You know very well it is unlawful for a Brahmin to shake hands with a ballet-master.

INDRU. But if I choose to lower myself to your level? I love one of the young ladies of your troupe.

CURRIE (*aside*). Another vacancy in my front row. (*aloud.*) A Nautch girl is no fit sweetheart for you. You must forget her.

INDRU. Forget her! I cannot. I think of her all day, and dream of her all night. Say what you like, she shall be my wife.

CURRIE (*aside*): Oh, shall she? I'm not going to have my troupe broken up into eligible marriage lots in this barefaced manner. (*aloud*). Listen to me. This lady is a member of the lowest caste, while you are of the highest, and the Hindu law distinctly says that persons of unequal rank may not marry under pain of death. The lady your Highness loves is my principal dancer, Hollee Beebee?

INDRU. Yes.

CURRIE. I thought so. Listen; I returned this morning with my troupe from a short provincial tour, and was met at the city gate by a chuprassie, who handed me a note from your father. He has heard of your infatuation, and commands me to put a stop to the affair at once, or——

INDRU. Or what?

CURRIE. He will cancel my music and dancing licence.

INDRU. What steps can *you* take in the matter?

CURRIE. Well, if a dancing master can't take steps, I should like to know who *can*. I shall command her to return your presents and letters forthwith.

INDRU. And if she refuse?

CURRIE. I shall fine her a week's salary. You'd better reconsider the matter. She's not the only girl in the world.

INDRU. She's the only girl in my heart.

DUET.—INDRU *and* CURRIE.

INDRU. Roses are fair, but not fairer than she,

CURRIE. Of feminine beauty beware, sir!

INDRU. Rubies are bright, but not brighter to me;

CURRIE. You see her without her back hair, sir.

INDRU. Sages are wise, but not wiser, I vow;

CURRIE. Her *h*'s she's always misplacing.

INDRU. Cutters are trim, but not trimmer; come now——

CURRIE. The fruits of incessant tight-lacing.

INDRU.   But be she plain, what do I care,
         So long as I believe her fair?
    It's simply a question of taste, you know,
         Simply a question of taste.
           This person's gladness
           Is that person's sadness,
         It's simply a question of taste.

CHORUS.   It's simply, &c.

INDRU.   Lilies are pure, but not purer than she ;

CURRIE.   She's more wide-a-wake than you think, sir,

INDRU.   Comrades are true, but not truer to me ;

CURRIE.   At strangers I've known her to wink, sir.

INDRU.   Willows are lithe, but not lither, you'll own ;

CURRIE.   All thanks to my excellent training.

INDRU.   Song birds are sweet, but not sweeter in tone ;

CURRIE.   She can't reach B flat without straining.

INDRU.   But be she *that*, well, what's amiss
         So long as I believe her *this?*

CHORUS.   It's simply, &c.

                     [*Exeunt* CURRIE *and* CHORUS.

INDRU. Is there no way by which I can marry Beebee? (*starting, with a sudden inspiration*). Stay! Could I not renounce my caste? The thing is simple enough. I have but to eat a little potted cow in public and it is done. Both of the same rank, we may marry, and none can separate us. What is caste compared with Beebee? I'll do it, and this very day she shall be mine for ever. (*Goes off.*)

Enter BANYAN, KALEE, TIFFIN, *and* NAUTCH GIRLS.

CHORUS.

    With merry song
    We trip along
Treading through the idle throng.
    While from our eyes
    The fire flies
That kindles hope in the unwise.
    We never woo
    As others do
With passion ardent, firm and true ;
    For we would stay
    Unwed for aye,
To love, and love, and run away.

SOLO.—BANYAN.

The monarch upon his throne
　　May hold a mighty sway ;
The sailor upon the sea
　　May chant a merry lay ;
The miser amidst his gold
　　May chuckle in his pride ;
The maiden upon the quay
　　May hail the coming tide.
But neither the monarch, nor sailor on sea,
Nor miser with gold, nor maiden on quay,
Are half so contented and happy as we.

CHORUS.　　　Contented and happy as we.

TIFFIN.　We call a crust a banquet, and a wail a roundelay,
　　That's our merry cakes and sherry, hey down derry way !

ALL.　　　We call a crust, &c.

SOLO.—KALEE.

The poet upon a hill
　　May dream a blissful dream ;
The cattle upon the lea
　　May lap the cooling stream ;
The children upon the mead
　　May skip in mirthful play ;
The sparrow upon the tree
　　May wake the sleeping day.
But neither the poet, nor cattle on lea,
Nor children on mead, nor sparrow on tree,
Are half so contented and happy as we.

CHORUS.　　　Contented and happy as we.

TIFFIN.　We call a cot a palace, and a cloud a golden ray,
　　That's our merry cakes and sherry, hey down derry way !

ALL.　　　We call a cot, &c.

Enter BEEBEE.

RECITATIVE.—BEEBEE.

And if you ask us whence this endless joy—
This happy lot—this bliss without alloy?
We answer, 'tis the guerdon of our art,
Which few attain, for few can play the part.

SONG—BEEBEE.

First you take a shapely maiden,
  Tall of stature, sweet of face,
Eyes with hidden mischief laden,
  Limbs that move with lissom grace;
Then you robe this charming creature,
  So her beauty to enhance;
Thus embellished, you may teach her
  All the movements of the dance.
    Shape the toe,
    Point it so,
    Hang the head,
    Arms outspread,
    Give the wrist
    Graceful twist,
    Eyes half-closed,
    Now you're posed.
And the rest is A, B, C;
Simply one, two, three.

INDRU *enters at back.*

INDRU (*advancing*).   Beebee!

BEEBEE (*runs to him—he puts his arm round her waist*).   Indru!
Remember the girls.

BANYAN.   Yes, remember the girls.

KALEE.   We're only human, you know.

TIFFIN.   And have our feelings.

INDRU.   I'm very sorry, ladies; but, really, your habit of always
travelling in a crowd is most embarrassing.   We don't at all mind
being left alone, if you've anything on.

BANYAN.   But we haven't.

INDRU.   Now, if you really *have* any appointments anywhere,
pray——

BANYAN.   We never make detached appointments.

TIFFIN.   We couldn't think of leaving Beebee unprotected.
Beebee wouldn't like it.

BEEBEE.   No, I shouldn't like it.   I should object.

KALEE.   We couldn't turn our thoughts away from Beebee under
any circumstances.

INDRU. But if you can't turn your thoughts away, you might see the propriety of turning your heads.

BEEBEE. Yes, girls, you might turn your heads.

BANYAN. If we are in the way you had better say so.

TIFFIN. We can take a hint.

INDRU. Oh, you *can* take a hint?

GIRLS. Yes.

INDRU. Then I wish to goodness you would take one. Take several; take a dozen; help yourselves to as many as you like, and go!

[*Girls go off sulkily.*

INDRU (*takes her by both hands*). Beebee, I have serious news. My father has discovered our secret. Oh, if you were only a Brahmin!

BEEBEE. I *am*; or rather, I *was*.

INDRU. I don't understand.

BEEBEE. Forty years ago my father, a respected Brahmin, was crossing a river; the boat capsized; a man on the bank threw a rope and hauled him ashore.

INDRU. And his life was saved?

BEEBEE. Yes; but his caste was lost.

INDRU. How so?

BEEBEE. The man on the bank was a Pariah, and the Court held that the taint of dishonour was communicated from him to my father down the rope.

INDRU. What a pity he didn't slip on a pair of gloves before grasping it.

BEEBEE. He appealed against the decision, and the case has been pending ever since. We were once a wealthy family, but all our possessions have been squandered in Court fees and legal refreshers. It was to pay for Counsel's opinion on a technical point that I took an engagement as a Nautch dancer.

INDRU. Brave girl! But why this endless delay?

BEEBEE. We have been most unfortunate. First of all, one of the Jury died, and they had to go through it all again; then our Counsel took the scarlet fever; and then, to vary the monotony, the Counsel on the other side took the yellow fever. Then one of the officials absconded with the brief; then they lost the shorthand notes; and so it has gone on for forty years.

INDRU. And is the Court still sitting?

BEEBEE. Yes, or rather, it was. The Judge has got the influenza now.

INDRU. It will be unfortunate if anything should happen to him. They would have to go through it all again, wouldn't they?

BEEBEE. Don't! The very suggestion makes me feel quite giddy (*cross.*)

INDRU. Do you think the case ever *will* end?

BEEBEE. I don't think it will (*sobs*).

INDRU (*confidentially*). Never mind—we will be married all the same.

BEEBEE. Impossible!

INDRU. Nothing is impossible to those who love as we love. If you cannot come up to my level, I must come down to yours.

DUET.—INDRU *and* BEEBEE.

INDRU.	When our shackles are undone, 　　When I breathe the word, Wilt thou have this man, fair one, 　　To thy wedded lord?
BEEBEE.	I will.
INDRU.	Wilt thou honour and obey him, 　　Never hoodwink or betray him? Wilt thou true allegiance pay him?
BEEBEE.	I will.
	In sickness and health, 　　In want and in wealth, I take thee for ever and ever.
	When the gossip-tongue's astir 　　With the Nautch girl's life, Wilt thou have this maiden, sir, 　　To thy wedded wife?
INDRU.	I will.
BEEBEE.	If unworthy they would make her, 　　If they ask thee to forsake her, Wilt thou to thy bosom take her?
INDRU.	I will. 　　In sunshine and rain, 　　In peace and in pain, I take thee for ever and ever.

Enter CURRIE.

CURRIE. Still at it. Are you aware, young lady, that you are braving the terrors of the law?

BEEBEE. What have I done?

CURRIE. Well, when a Nautch girl aspires to the hand of a Prince, I think you will admit she's done something.

BEEBEE. But I was not aware of his rank when I fell in love with him.

CURRIE. Then you should have inquired. You don't expect a member of the Royal Family to go about with a crown on his head and a throne in his portmanteau, do you? Now see the result. The Rajah has ordered you to be brought before him for trial, and you will probably be sentenced to be thrown to the sacred crocodiles (BEEBEE cries).

INDRU (aside to BEEBEE). Be brave, Beebee. I will return in five minutes to claim you as my own, and not even the Rajah can then separate us. [Exit.

CURRIE (earnestly). I may be able to save you.

BEEBEE. Yes?

CURRIE. I have arranged to take my troupe to the Paris Exhibition, and am expecting the signed agreement every moment. A steamer sails in an hour's time, and if the contract arrives before then we can all get on board and escape.

BEEBEE. And leave Indru? No.

CURRIE. Foolish girl! Come with me—not that way! (trying to pull her off). Here comes the Rajah! (he takes her off).

CHORUS.

Room for Punka, room for Punka,
  Punka comes in Royal state!
Clear the roadway, clear the roadway,
  Punka comes, Punka the Great!
Crash the cymbal, beat the tom-tom,
  Let the brazen trumpet roar;
Room for Punka, Royal Punka,
  Rajah he of Chutneypore!

Enter PUNKA.

RECITATIVE.

PUNKA. Oh, yes! oh, yes! oh, yes! Know all men by these presents, I'm the Rajah of Chutneypore!

CHORUS. Punka, the Rajah of Chutneypore, the Rajah of Chutneypore!

SONG.

PUNKA.   And this is the royal diadem
          Of the Rajah of Chutneypore.

CHORUS.   Of Punka, of Punka, the Rajah of Chutneypore,

PUNKA.   And this is the big ancestral gem
          That decks the royal diadem
          Of the Rajah of Chutneypore.

CHORUS.   Of Punka, &c.

PUNKA.   And this is the arm all cut and scored
          That wields the sharp and trusty sword,
          That guards the big ancestral gem
          That decks the royal diadem
          Of the Rajah of Chutneypore.

CHORUS.   Of Punka, &c.

PUNKA.   And this is the heart so staunch and true,
          That nerves the eye of hazel hue,
          That steers the arm all cut and scored,
          That wields the sharp and trusty sword,
          That guards the big ancestral gem
          That decks the royal diadem
          Of the Rajah of Chutneypore.

CHORUS.   Of Punka, &c.

PUNKA.   And this is the Prince, long may he reign,
          That owns the clear and subtle brain,
          That rules the heart so staunch and true,
          That nerves the eye of hazel hue,
          That steers the arm all cut and scored,
          That wields the sharp and trusty sword,
          That guards the big ancestral gem
          That decks the royal diadem
          Of the Rajah of Chutneypore.

CHORUS.   Of Punka, &c.

PUNKA.   And this is the patriotic lay
          That's sung by the lords and ladies gay
          That serve the Prince, long may he reign,
          That owns the clear and subtle brain,
          That rules the heart so staunch and true,
          That nerves the eye of hazel hue,
          That steers the arm all cut and scored,
          That wields the sharp and trusty sword,
          That guards the big ancestral gem
          That decks the royal diadem
          Of the Rajah of Chutneypore.

CHORUS.   Of Punka, &c.

PUNKA. Well, where is our cousin—the active and intelligent Pyjama?

Enter PYJAMA, *followed by* BEEBEE.

PUNKA. Oh, here you are! (*To* PYJAMA). And where is this Nautch girl who has dared to make love to our son?—(*warming up*)—this creature who has, as it were, presumed, so to speak, even so much as to—but we'll take it as read. Where is she?

PYJAMA. Here, your Highness (*brings forward* BEEBEE, *who kneels*).

PUNKA. Ha! (*advances furiously to her*). Now, young person, hold up your head!

BANYAN. Poor Beebee!

PUNKA. Silence, or I'll clear the Court. (*To* BEEBEE) Hold up your head! Hold up your head, I say! Will you hold up—(*she looks up, he suddenly melts and smiles at her*).

PUNKA. How d'ye do? Warm, isn't it? (*aside*). What a pretty face! I'm not at all surprised at Indru. How lovely!

PYJAMA (*stepping in front of him, admiring* BEEBEE). Charming!

PUNKA (*aside*). Now, were it not for the consanguinity existing between myself and that person, I should peremptorily order them to cleave him through the skull. (*aloud*). Ahem! (PYJAMA *moves—* PUNKA *raises* BEEBEE). And so you love my little Indy, eh, pretty one?

BEEBEE. Yes, your Highness.

PUNKA. And did it not occur to you that such presumption on the part of a Nautch girl would rouse the ire of the mildest monarch that ever lived?

BEEBEE. I was not aware of his exalted rank, your Highness, or I would not have dared to look at him.

PUNKA. I should think not, indeed. Our family are not only Brahmins, but Brahmins of the very finest vintage. We have been in bottle, so to speak, eighteen hundred years. I think I am justified in saying that you have not even a *trace* of blue in your veins.

BEEBEE. I don't know, your Highness.

PUNKA. Look at that! (*gives paper*). It is a chemical analysis of our family blood, which, you will observe, yields one hundred and twenty grains of indigo to the square inch.

BEEBEE. How very blue it must be!

PUNKA. It is—unusually blue.

PYJAMA (*idiotically*). I reckon one of us would be of incalculable value to a family who do their washing at home.

PUNKA (*to* PYJAMA, *glaring at him*). Idiot! (*to* BEEBEE) You will now understand that the difference between my son's rank and your own is a complete bar to your union.

BEEBEE. I do, your Highness.

PUNKA. Then you are a sensible girl, and that fact will be taken into consideration when the Court proceeds to pass judgment upon you.

BEEBEE. I am conscious of my crime, your Highness, and at your feet I crave your mercy (*kneels, weeping*).

PUNKA (*aside*). How pretty she looks through her tears! (*stooping over her*). Dry your eyes, sweet one, dry your eyes.

PYJAMA (*passing in front of him*). Allow me, miss.

PUNKA. Ahem! (PYJAMA *falls back—aside*). If he were not a relation—— (*aloud*). In consideration of your deep contrition, you will be merely required to enter into your own recognizances for your future good conduct. The Court has been moved to take this lenient view of the case on account of the prisoner's extreme youth and beauty, and we wish it to go forth—and possibly the gentlemen of the press will take note of it—I say, we wish it to go forth, that if only the prisoner were a Brahmin, we should not be at all averse to receiving her into our family, either as a daughter—or wife——

PYJAMA (*embracing* BEEBEE). Or cousin.

PUNKA (*aside*). I shall certainly give that person a sound thrashing one day, relative or no relative. (*aloud*). The prisoner leaves the Court without a stain on her character.

(*Exeunt to refrain of Chorus* PYJAMA, BEEBEE, BANYAN, KALEE, TIFFIN, *and* CHORUS. PUNKA *remains*.)

PUNKA. Thank goodness! they're all gone.

CHINNA *enters*.

CHINNA. What, Rajah! all alone? You seem annoyed.

PUNKA. I believe I am the most unfortunate monarch on earth, and all owing to the pernicious influence of a certain phrenological bump (*feels his skull*).

CHINNA. Nonsense!

PUNKA. No; not nonsense. Consanguinity—there it is! (*indicates the organ*).

CHINNA. There isn't such a bump.

PUNKA. There wasn't until I was born. I was the first to develop it. It is now over four years since I communicated my discovery to the *Lancet;* and they were good enough to christen the new organ, "Consanguinity, No. 39 A."

CHINNA. And what has this to do with your ill fate?

PUNKA. Everything. If the love of kindred had not predominated in my composition to such an absurd degree, I should never have taken you and Pyjama from the gutter—metaphorically speaking—and put you in office at Court. From that unfortunate act all my troubles date; for no sooner had it become known that I was recognizing my poor relations, than cousins, half-cousins, quarter-cousins, and fractions of cousins turned up from every quarter of Hindustan; until at the present moment there isn't a single post in my kingdom—to which a salary is attached—that isn't held by one of them.

CHINNA. They ought to be grateful.

PUNKA. You catch them being grateful! They're always asking for something, and they're never satisfied until they've got it, and *then* they're not. Oh, I wish they were all in the crocodile pond.

CHINNA. Why doesn't your Majesty *put* them there—with exceptions, of course. You have but to command your guards.

PUNKA. Yes, I can command my guards, but can I command my feelings? The rascals remind me that the "same blood flows in our veins." Ugh! I know they're a lot of sponging, treacherous humbugs, and yet the same old arguments always fetch me.

CHINNA. But, your Majesty——

PUNKA. Don't interrupt, please. Then there's this bother about Indru—and that tiresome business of the diamond too.

CHINNA. But that wasn't a relation's doing, was it?

PUNKA (*mysteriously*). It was. Ten years ago one of them, who shall be nameless——(*looks off after* PYJAMA).

CHINNA (*astonished*). Pyjama?

PUNKA. Never mind; whoever it was, he stole the diamond that formed the left eye of Bumbo, the Idol, and sold it to an Englishman, who travelled in curios for a London firm. We instantly despatched a High Priest and a couple of Thugs to recover the precious jewel. They pursued it through many vicissitudes, but missed it at every turn. They traced it first to the diamond merchant in Hatton Garden; but the day before they arrived, his safe had been broken open, and the diamond stolen by a well-to-do burglar, who, for better security, deposited it at his banker's, whose head cashier promptly absconded with the Idol's eye in his portmanteau to Spain. On the journey the train was robbed by a party of brigands, whose leader, a fine, fearless, free-shooting fellow, was about to start for the Spanish Exhibition at Earl's Court, of which he was to be one of the chief attractions. He ultimately became a lion of the London season, and gave the diamond to a Countess, whose husband, being dissatisfied with her story that she found it in the folds of her train after a scrimmage at a drawing-room at Buckingham Palace, flung it in a rage out of his back bed-room window into a mews, where it was picked up and swallowed by an enterprising Cochin China fowl, who was killed next day. It was discovered by the cook in dressing the bird; she gave it to a policeman, who gave it to a housemaid, who gave it to a Life-Guardsman, who gave it to a pretty parlour-maid, who gave it to a young gentleman just home from Eton, against whom she soon afterwards entered an action for breach of promise. After a vain attempt to convince the Court that his letters had been written by a foster-brother of whom he was the identical image, the youth fled with the diamond to other climes. He was last heard of in the interior of Africa, where he has evaded our emissaries, and twice escaped being " rescued " by private expeditions sent out by the English. Since then, all trace of him has been lost.

CHINNA. Then nothing can be done?

PUNKA. What more do you want? I am held responsible by the outraged Idol for the absence of his optic. The terror is always over me. You don't know what an irritable, despotic deity this Bumbo is. There's absolutely no knowing what he may take it into his head to do, or what time he may choose for doing it. Unless I can find the jewel, or find it in my heart to denounce a relative, I fear the worst.

CHINNA. But why *did* you not denounce the thief?

PUNKA. You know my unfortunate weakness. He fell on his knees and said, "Am I not your fifty-fifth cousin?" (*aside*). Ah here is the rascal!

PYJAMA *enters, bringing on* BEEBEE.

PYJAMA. The young person has a communication to make.

BEEBEE. Your Highness was good enough to say that if I were a Brahmin you would accept me as your daughter—

PUNKA. Or wife—

BEEBEE. I *am* of Brahmin descent, and am now petitioning the Court to restore my lost rank.

PUNKA. If you succeed, you may call at our Palace any Monday morning between ten and twelve; and if our son is by that time married, and we are still a widower, we will give you the refusal of our hand and heart.

BEEBEE. Your Majesty is too good.

PUNKA. Not at all. I have been looking for a wife for some time; you come up to my idea of what a wife should be; and as such, you would, I think, supply a long-felt want.

QUARTET.

PUNKA.   Now, when a young man says, "I think
         It's time I lost my heart,"
     He ought to look around, I think,
         Before he throws the dart.
     For model wives and true, I think,
     Are far between and few, I think ;
     Though there are odd ones who, I think,
         Supply a long-felt want.

Not the bilious-headache person who sits moping in a chair,
Nor the Senior-Wrangler person with a stubble crop of hair,
Nor the Bloom of Ninon person whose face won't stand the weather,
But quite another different kind of person altogether.

ALL.   Yes, quite another, &c.

BEEBEE.   And when a maiden says, "I think
         I'll let him buy the ring,"
     She ought to ask herself, I think,
         "Now, is he quite the thing ?"
     For model men and fair, I think,
     Are very, very rare, I think,
     Yet one may here and there, I think,
         Supply a long-felt want.

Not the third-class-smoking person who is colouring a clay,
Nor the ten-in-fifty person who plays billiards all the day,
Nor the tea-and-muffin person who will strike you with a feather,
But quite another different kind of person altogether.

ALL.   Yes, quite another, &c.

PYJAMA.   This maxim will apply, I think,
         To old as well as young ;
     And when December woos, I think,
         He ought to guard his tongue.
     For model wives and good, I think,
     Are rare in widowhood, I think,
     Yet there are some who would, I think,
         Supply a long-felt want.

Not the breach-of-promise person who salutes each man she sees,
Nor the House of Commons person who wants feminine M.P.'s,
Nor the Hallelujah person whose lungs are made of leather,
But quite another different kind of person altogether.

ALL.   Yes, quite another, &c.

CHINNA.   The sauce that suits the goose, I think,
        Should suit the gander too ;
    And Joan should have a care, I think,
        When Darby comes to woo.
    For model men and old, I think,
    Are rare on earth as gold, I think,
    Though odd ones, I've been told, I think,
        Supply a long-felt want.

Not the sluggish-liver person who says just what he feels,
Nor the extra-special person who *will* read through all his meals,
Nor the atmospheric person who changes with the weather,
But quite another different kind of person altogether.

ALL.   Yes, quite another, &c.

Enter INDRU, *wearing the dress of an outcast.*

PUNKA (*seeing* INDRU, *who salaams*). Indru, what means this?

INDRU. I am no longer a Brahmin, your Majesty.

PUNKA. Is this a joke?

INDRU. No, sir. I have just eaten a small plate of potted cow in the Bazaar, and renounced my caste. So now I may marry Beebee, sweet Beebee !

CHINNA (*aside*). To think that he should throw himself away like this ; and just when it had suddenly struck me that he was the one person capable of making me happy !

PUNKA. What right have you to do such a thing? You have cut yourself off from me for ever.

CHINNA. And from me.

PYJAMA. And from me, and all your cousins.

INDRU. I can only plead my love in extenuation.

PUNKA. Here am I, in the autumn of life, without a son to cheer my declining years, without an heir to inherit my crown. What is to be done ?

PYJAMA. May I suggest a scheme ?

PUNKA. Have you a vested interest in it ?

PYJAMA. Well, er—yes, slightly.

PUNKA. I thought so. We don't want to hear it.

[*Exit* PYJAMA.

INDRU (*aside to* BEEBEE). I have prepared everything. They waiting now to marry us. Come !

[BEEBEE *and* INDRU *steal off.*

(PUNKA *sits, deeply depressed.*)

CHINNA (*coming up to him and putting her hand on his shoulder*). Cheer up, Rajah! you are not the only unhappy being whose feelings get the best of him. I, too, am a victim of irresistible impulses.

PUNKA. You?

CHINNA. Since I was sixteen I have been seeking for my affinity, that mysterious being who is waiting for me somehow, somewhere.

PUNKA. Where?

CHINNA. I don't exactly know where.

PUNKA. Oh, I thought perhaps it was an appointment.

CHINNA. Whenever I meet him a thrill passes over me. I see nothing, hear nothing, smell nothing, taste nothing, feel nothing.

PUNKA. I say, I *say!* That's very bad.

CHINNA. Please, don't interrupt me, Rajah. I mean, of course, except *him!*

PUNKA. And are these indications invariably accurate?

CHINNA. Well, on one or two occasions, certainly I have mistaken the symptoms; but I see you do not understand me.

SONG.—CHINNA.

(*Words by Frank Desprez.*)

Do not think me over-bold,
　　Though my sentiments are strong;
And my heart is far from cold—
　　Well, in that there's nothing wrong.
　　　I am seeking my divinity,
　　　My idol, my affinity;
And when I come across him—as I often think I do—
　　　I forget myself a minute,
　　　But there's really nothing in it.

PUNKA.　　Have you often had these " impulses "?

CHINNA.　　That's most unkind of *you!*

(*Refrain.*)　I can't help it! Really no!
Do not laugh—'tis truly so.
On each of these occasions,
These passing aberrations,
My heart goes out to meet him,
And my arms extend to greet him—
To a kiss I'd almost treat him.
　　　I can't help it!

CHINNA. These attacks, I'm glad to mention,
　　Only last a little while,
　I return to stern convention,
　　To a sneer subdue my smile.
　　　Avoid familiarity,
　　　Snub ordinary charity,
　And freeze him with a frown that keeps him off a yard or two.
　　　Atone for past frivolity
　　　By speech of coldest quality.

PUNKA. Do you often ice your manner?

CHINNA. Now that's much too bad of you!

(*Refrain*.)　I can't help it, really no!
　　Through the world I sadly go.
　　　I am seeking a divinity,
　　　And finding an affinity,
　　My heart goes out to meet him,
　　And my arms extend to greet him,
　　To a kiss I'd almost treat him,
　　　I can't help it!

[*Exit* CHINNA.

PYJAMA *enters*.

PUNKA. Well, what is it now?

PYJAMA (*with suppressed delight*). I've some more news for you,
Beebee's action is finished. The Court has decided in her favour,
and she is now a Brahmin.

PUNKA. A Brahmin! And just as Indru has renounced his
caste! Now, could there possibly be anything more exasperating.

PYJAMA. It certainly has its humorous side, hasn't it?

PUNKA. They're as far from marriage as ever.

PYJAMA. Poor girl! But she sha'n't be disappointed of a wedding!

PUNKA. How so?

PYJAMA. I'll marry her myself.

[*Exit.*

PUNKA. And I believe he would. I honestly think that man's
capable of anything.

[*Exit.*

FINALE.

Enter BANJAN, KALEE, TIFFIN, *Nautch Girls, Soldiers, and others.*

CHORUS OF NAUTCH GIRLS.

Merrily, merrily peals the bell,
  In the temple swinging;
Merrily, merrily voices swell,
  Gladsome tidings bringing.
Merrily, merrily press the crowd,
  From Beebee's wedding we come;
Merrily, merrily chant aloud
  Her epithalamium.

Enter INDRU *and* BEEBEE.

BEEBEE.	Beebee's a bride now, as every one knows,
INDRU.	And Beebee's all blushes, just like a red rose.
BEEBEE.	Beebee is trembling with maidenly fears,
INDRU.	And Beebee is smiling, in spite of her tears.
BEEBEE.	Beebee is glowing with womanly pride,
INDRU.	And Beebee's the sweetest and handsomest bride.
BEEBEE.	Beebee is beaming with conjugal mirth,
INDRU.	And Beebee's the happiest creature on earth.

PUNKA *and* PYJAMA *have entered.* PUNKA *comes forward.*

PUNKA.   Oh, headstrong pair, your folly you will rue,
          The Court has issued its award, and you (*to* BEEBEE)
          Are now a Brahmin.

(*Gives paper—pause—horror of* INDRU *and* BEEBEE.)

                By the law's decree
Your vows are void; his wife you ne'er can be.

PUNKA, INDRU, PYJAMA.

Stop the merry marriage bell,
  Hush the joyous song;
Toll instead the dolesome knell,
  Beat the mystic gong.
Haul the silken banners down,
  Halt the pageant show;
Doff the smile and don the frown,
  Chant the hymn of woe.   (*All repeat.*)

SOLO.—INDRU.

What is caste to you and me,
  Who live for love alone?
To some country let us flee,
  Where no such bann is known.

To some far-off happy land
  ·Beyond the Brahmin's sway,
We will journey hand in hand,
  To live and love for aye.

BEEBEE.   Yes, yes, that happy land we'll find,
    And leave this hated caste behind.

CHORUS.   That happy, happy land they'll find,
    And leave this hated caste behind.

SOLO.—PYJAMA.

One moment pause.   My conscience bids me throw
A cloud across the sunshine of your hopes.
It is decreed by Act of Punka Rex,
19 & 20, Cap. 18, that when
A Brahmin marries one of lower caste,
Together they shall die a traitor's death.
And kinsfolk, loving kinsfolk though you be,
My conscience bids me go for the police.,

        [*Exit* PYJAMA, *followed by* PUNKA.

CHORUS.   Oh, cruel law ! oh, harsh decree !
      Oh, statute born of fool !
    Oh, fiendish code ! oh, carrion rite !
      Oh, legislative ghoul !

INDRU.   Must we then die ?   Is there no hope left still ?

BEEBEE.   Can no one save us ?

CURRIE (*entering*).   Yes, I can and will !

SOLO.—CURRIE.

The ship is waiting by the quay
To bear my troupe across the sea.
And here's the contract, which you'll find
Is duly stamped and sealed and signed.
So come with me and join my band,
And fly unto a foreign land,
And say farewell for evermore
To cross and cruel Chutneypore.

INDRU *and* BEEBEE.   Yes, yes, we'll go.

CURRIE.   Then do not longer wait.

INDRU.   Good-bye, farewell.

CURRIE.   Quick, ere it is too late.

BANYAN.	THE OTHERS.
Away, away,	Away, away
Ill-fated twain,	Across the main,
Whose wedding day	Beyond the sway
Is born in pain;	Of Brahma's reign,
Seek some lone spot	Unto a spot
Far o'er the sea.	Far o'er the sea,
May such a lot	Where caste is not
Ne'er come to me.	And men are free.

(CURRIE *hurries* BEEBEE *off.* INDRU *is about to follow her when*
PYJAMA *enters with Soldiers, who arrest him.*)

ACT II.

The Courtyard of PUNKA'S *Palace. A cell is seen, with grated window, in which* INDRU *is confined.* SUTTEE, CHEETAH, *and Poor Relations discovered.*

OPENING CHORUS.

We are Punka's poor relations
    By a lucky zephyr blown
Up the easiest gradations
    From the gutter to the throne.
We have risen from the people
    By a mighty strength of will,
From the basement to the steeple,
    From the valley to the hill.

Enter CHINNA.

SOLO.—CHINNA.

Not many years have journeyed by
Since we were of the common fry,
Governesses, teachers, nurses,
Lady-helps with slender purses,
Toiling, broiling, day by day
In a common, humdrum way—
Quite a common, humdrum way.
When Punka driven into meekness,
By some strange phrenologic weakness,
Summoned all his poor relations
From their low and humble station
Gave them posts about his throne,
And bade them make his home their own.

CHORUS.   We quickly made his home our own.

CHINNA.   And now our cousin rues the hour
When he invested us with power.
We rule the roast.   For truth to tell
He gave an inch, we took an ell.

SUTTEE.   Yes, yes, we took several ells.

CHEETAH.   An unlimited number of ells.

CHORUS.   Millions, and billions, and trillions, quadrillions, and
             also quintillions of ells!

CHINNA. And now we are ladies attached to the Court,
The highly-exclusive and towering sort;
With pinnacle people we only resort,
Like the high-top-gallant ladies that we are.

CHORUS. Yes, now we are, &c.

Enter PYJAMA *at back.*

PYJAMA. Well, cousins, the Court has pronounced its sentence. Indru is to die to-morrow.

CHINNA. To-morrow! (*aside*). I am only just in time.

CHEETAH. After lying six months in that prison! (*pointing*). Poor fellow!

CHINNA (*aside*). I wish they'd all go away!

SUTTEE. Poor Beebee!

CHINNA (*contemptuously*). Beebee! Who thinks of Beebee now? Since she and Currie's troupe escaped to Europe, they have been forgotten.

CHEETAH. We have read of them in the papers, and heard what successes they made in Paris and London.

SUTTEE. And what a lot of beautiful presents were sent them!

PYJAMA. Never mind about Beebee! Listen; I have communicated the facts about Indru and Punka in an anonymous letter to the Idol Bumbo, which I have laid on his shrine. When he learns that Punka is the father of a condemned outcast, he will certainly sentence *him* to die also! (*chuckling*).

CHINNA. And then you expect to be made Rajah! *I* know! (*goes up and gets off during song*).

CHEETAH. You seem to have arranged things splendidly for yourself—as usual.

PYJAMA. Would you like to know the secret of my luck?

CHEETAH *and* SUTTEE. We should.

GIRLS. Yes.

SONG.—PYJAMA.

The secret of my past success is simple in its way:
I carefully avoid unlucky actions night and day.
I never pared my finger-nails on Friday in my life;
I'd rather cross the river Styx than cross a table-knife;
I never from my house turned out a black-haired pussy-cat;
And when I meet a squint-eyed girl I always go like that!
And if I see a hunch-back pass, I touch him when I'm able,

And never since the innocent days of childhood have I ever so far forgotten myself as to put my boots upon the table.

CHORUS. And never since the innocent days of childhood, &c.

PYJAMA. 'Gainst thirteen round a table I instinctively revolt ;
"Self-help " is e'er my motto if I'm asked to give some salt ;
I wouldn't see a new moon through a glass for anything ;
I always turn my money when I hear the cuckoo sing ;
I never, never pass another person on the stairs,
Nor poke the fire unless I've known the owner seven years ;
I never whistle in a room, for nothing could be madder,
And I invariably step out into the roadway and risk amputation by the wheels of a passing vehicle rather than walk beneath a painter's ladder.

CHORUS. And he invariably steps, &c.

PYJAMA. I'm always very careful not to break a looking-glass ;
And when the train's going o'er a bridge beneath I never pass ;
I wouldn't wear a peacock's feather on my hat, oh, no !
Nor into a new domicile on Friday ever go.
And when I make a present, I by no chance give a knife ;
I've never stepped from bed upon the wrong side in my life ;
Than rather meet a funeral, I'd curl up in the gutter,
And be the craving of the inner man ever so acute, no living soul could on any account prevail upon me to take the last piece of bread and butter.

CHORUS. And be the craving, &c.

PYJAMA. When shaking hands I'm very, very careful not to cross ;
I always wish for something when I meet a piebald "hoss";
I wouldn't open an umbrella in a room for gold,
Nor have a baby photographed before it's six months old ;
On Twelfth-cake Day the mistletoe must always disappear,
And I engage a dark man to let in the glad new year ;
A black pin I would never use, for nothing could be bolder,
And if, in an unguarded moment, I'm ever betrayed into committing any of the aforementioned offences, I immediately propitiate the Fates by simply turning round three times, and tossing a pinch of salt over my left shoulder.

CHORUS. And if, in an unguarded moment, &c.

PYJAMA. Now, cousins, let us go and book seats for Indru's execution to-morrow.

PYJAMA *and others exeunt.* CHINNA *re-enters from back.*

CHINNA. At last they're gone—now is my chance. The bar and
the disguise that I have hidden (*looks for them behind
column*)—both safe! Indru—my affinity—that is, my
latest affinity—you can now escape!

DUET.—CHINNA *and* INDRU.

(Words by George Dance and Frank Desprez.)

A little caged bird below
A palace window hung;
His weary heart was crushed with woe,
And mute his silver tongue;
And ev'ry morn his faithful mate
Came from her lonesome nest,
And sang outside his prison-gate
The song he loved the best.

I'm waiting here below, she sang;
Why do you linger so? she sang;
'Tis I, my love, 'tis I, she sang,
And waited his reply (*listens*).

INDRU. I come—oh, do not go, my love;
The hours seem sad and slow, my love;
I'm weary of this woe, my love,
A captive held am I!
Well, pretty Chinna, have you come once more
To cheer the captive with your tuneful strain;
Useless your thought for such a wretch as I;
To-morrow—yes, to-morrow—I must die!

CHINNA. I've come to save you from your fate.
INDRU. But how
Save me? Alas! how can you save me now?
CHINNA (*showing it*). This bar of steel will break your prison-bars.
INDRU. 'Tis heavy; you can hardly lift its weight!
CHINNA. How can we get it up? Ah! let down straight
Your turban. (*He does so.*)
INDRU. Clever girl!
CHINNA. Haul up!
INDRU. I do!
CHINNA. Take that bar of trusty steel,
Ply it with a lusty zeal,
Burst your bonds, and you are free,
Oh, delicious liberty!

INDRU (*as he breaks bar*).

> Again, again,
> Each muscle I strain!
> The mortar is old!
> The bricks will not break!
> These bars still hold!
> No, no, they shake!
> They quiver, they bend!
> My task's at an end!
> 'Tis done! I am free! (*comes down.*)
> Thanks, Chinna, to thee!

(He gets out, and down stage.)

ENSEMBLE.

What joy to $\left\{\begin{array}{l}\text{him,}\\\text{me,}\end{array}\right\}$ what joy to $\left\{\begin{array}{l}\text{him!}\\\text{me!}\end{array}\right\}$

What happiness to break $\left\{\begin{array}{l}\text{his}\\\text{one's}\end{array}\right\}$ chain!

Oh, welcome, sweetest liberty!

$\left.\begin{array}{l}\text{He's}\\\text{I'm}\end{array}\right\}$ free again, $\left\{\begin{array}{l}\text{he's}\\\text{I'm}\end{array}\right\}$ free again!

INDRU. And now, dear Chinna, I must fly.

CHINNA. Not so.

> You must not in that garb attempt to go.
> Here (*showing it*) is a dress in which, when once
>   disguised,
> You will not, I believe, be recognized!

INDRU. Is there aught more?

CHINNA. Nothing—unless—
You——

INDRU. What?

CHINNA (*aside*). How dense men are! (*aloud*) Why, can't you
  guess?
> I want to leave this hateful Chutneypore,
> And never see this palace any more,
> Beebee has left you—she is not your wife—
> And, if you asked me to be yours for life,
> Perhaps I'd not refuse—

INDRU. What can I say?
> Would that this heart were mine to give away!
> And then—but, no—Beebee is still my own,
> And, though we're parted, I am hers alone!

BOTH.   This is the old, old story! Jack is in love with Jill;
  Jill doesn't care for Johnny, but deeply adoreth Bill;
  Bill worships dainty Dorothy—Dorothy, trim and tall,
  Is pining and burning for Dick, who is yearning
  For Cis, who loves no one at all.

CHINNA (*aside*). Another disappointment; Well, I'm used to it
Sooner or later I shall find him—later probably. (*aloud.*) But
you've no time to lose—on with that disguise, and——

INDRU (*pointing off* R.).   Look, my father! I must say farewell
to him.

CHINNA. Impossible! (*pointing* L.) See! That horrid Pyjama,
He will certainly betray you! Round this corner, quick!

[*Exit* INDRU.

CHINNA. The next time I find my affinity there shall be no
mistake about it.

[*Exit* CHINNA.

Enter PUNKA, *pensively*, R.

PUNKA. More troubles!

Enter PYJAMA, *running*.

PYJAMA. Have you heard the news?

PUNKA. What news?

PYJAMA. Of Bumbo the Idol.

PUNKA. Bumbo?

PYJAMA. He has come to life.

PUNKA. Ha! That's so like him. Just the sort of thing he
would do. Pure aggravation!

PYJAMA. Yes. (*Melodramatic music.*) As one of the Priests of the
Temple was dusting him this morning, he noticed a wave of animation slowly passing over his face.

PUNKA. Ha!

PYJAMA. His lips quivered, his nostrils dilated, and then his one
eye slowly opened like the moon emerging from a cloud.

PUNKA. Ha!

PYJAMA. He gave one mighty shiver, stretched his arms, yawned
three times, and, after wiping a cobweb from the corner of his
eye, stepped from the shelf on which he has been sitting for two
thousand years. (*Music stops.*)

PUNKA. What's he doing now?

PYJAMA. He is coming *here!*   [*Exeunt separately.*

Enter SUTTEE, CHEETAH, *Poor Relations, and Priests*

CHORUS.

PRIESTS.   Oh, ye people! Oh, ye people!
        Cast yourselves upon the earth;
      Grovel, grovel, creep and grovel,
        So confess your humble worth!

GIRLS.   Bumbo comes! The mighty Bumbo!
        Brahma's idol, great and just;
      Grovel, grovel, man and maiden,
        Bow the head and lick the dust!

Enter BUMBO, *carried on by Priests in a sedan chair. The doors are suddenly thrown open, and he steps out. He has the appearance of having been recently gilded and varnished, and wears a green shade over his left eye.*

RECITATIVE.—BUMBO.

'Tis well! 'tis well! Your piety I praise,
Remain and bask in mighty Bumbo's rays.
You marvel doubtless at my animation,
I'll condescend e'en to an explanation.

SONG.—BUMBO.

(Words by Frank Desprez.)

As I sat on my shelf, alone all by myself,
    What Idol so happy as I?
I could see what went on, who had come, who was gone,
    And the slightest omission espy.
Not an offering placed on the altar that graced
    My temple was ever unseen,
Though my right eye was dim, yet the fellow to him
    Was a gem of the purest, serene.
        And how do you think,
          The trouble arose,
        That left me no wink
          Of my pleasant repose?

CHORUS.   It was all his eye—

BUMBO.   It was all my eye,

CHORUS.   The diamond eye,

BUMBO.   My diamond eye,

CHORUS.   It was all his eye,

BUMBO.   My brilliant eye!

CHORUS.   The diamond eye of the Idol!

One day to the shrine which you visit as mine
    There came an irreverent tramp,
Religion forgetting, my eye from its setting
    He whipped—'twas the left, too, the scamp !
You often may wonder what's causing the thunder,
    Though cloudless the heavens may be ;
Don't notice the rumbling, it's only me grumbling
    To think that the villain's still free.

        And why do I rage,
          Vituperate,
        What is the reason
          My wrath's so great ?

CHORUS.	It's all his eye,
BUMBO.	It was all my eye,
CHORUS.	The diamond eye,
BUMBO.	My diamond eye,
CHORUS.	It was all his eye,
BUMBO.	My long-lost eye, my envied eye,
	My kidnapped eye, my brilliant eye,

BUMBO *and* CHORUS.   The diamond eye of the Idol !

BUMBO (*to* PUNKA). Well, Punka, you didn't expect me, eh ? Have you made your will ?

PUNKA. My will ?

BUMBO. You're very dense this morn ing ! I'll put it another way Have you anything to say why sentence of death should not be passed upon you ?

PUNKA. Sentence of death ? My dear boy——

BUMBO. Don't address me as your dear boy. I'm not a boy ; I celebrated my two-thousandth birthday last week.

PUNKA. But——

BUMBO. Silence ! You have a son who a few months ago renounced his caste by eating potted cow ?

PUNKA. Potted cow ? But that's not me !

BUMBO. The enactment is retrospective. The same cow—I mean the same blood—runs——

PUNKA. Not *that* argument ; I can't bear it ! I hear it so often.

BUMBO. He has been sentenced to death for marrying out of his caste. A felon's father cannot reign here. You have violated the sanctity of the throne.

PUNKA. But, surely, you attach no weight to the mad actions of a love-smitten youth?

BUMBO. I attach a weight to anything that serves my purpose. I shall presently attach a weight to your neck, preparatory to hurling you into the crocodiles' pond.

PYJAMA. Hear, hear!

POOR RELA. Hear, hear!

PRIESTS. Hear, hear!

BUMBO. And then (*savagely*)—what about my eye?

PUNKA. How could I prevent some person (*looking at* PYJAMA, *who winces*), who shall be nameless, from stealing it? I have acted as your guardian for many years, and, with this exception, you will allow I have proved faithful to my trust?

BUMBO. I allow nothing!

PUNKA. I took you from my father on a repairing lease, didn't I?

BUMBO. You did.

PUNKA. And I have done all to you that has been necessary, have I not?

BUMBO. In a jerry-built way, yes.

PUNKA. Haven't I had you insured against fire for three times your value?

BUMBO. After quietly abstracting the premium from the missionary-box.

PUNKA. When once a party of British tourists cut their initials on your nose, didn't I immediately have them obliterated?

BUMBO. With putty—ugh! I can smell it now!

PUNKA. Didn't I have you painted and gilded up two years ago?

BUMBO. Not gilded, Dutch-metalled.

PUNKA. And give you three coats of the best oak varnish in the spring?

BUMBO. You did, and I've been sticky ever since, confound you! I'm a perfect catch-'em-alive-oh! Where is your son?

PUNKA. In yonder prison.

BUMBO. Produce him!

PYJAMA. Ha, look! (*points to bars*) The bars are forced! The prisoner has flown!

BUMBO. Guard the city gates! (*To* PUNKA) You are Rajah no longer. Go, exchange that royal robe for the garb of an out-cast, and return here prepared for your doom!

PUNKA. Would you leave the people without a leader?

PYJAMA (*stepping forward*). Don't make yourself anxious about that. (*To* BUMBO) As Grand Vizier, I understand the duties of

Rajah well, and am quite prepared to accept the situation on the usual salary.

PUNKA. Ungrateful dog!

BUMBO. Take him away!

[*Exit* PUNKA *guarded.*

(*To* PYJAMA). I appoint you Rajah in his stead. Within half an hour you will throw them, father and son, into the sacred water.

PYJAMA. Your commands shall be obeyed.

BUMBO. Mind they are! You can't deceive me. The moment they are seized by the hungry reptiles I shall be made aware of the fact by a pleasant tickling sensation on the soles of my feet, and if that titillation be delayed one instant beyond the stated time, then beware of the vengeance of the mighty Bumbo! (*aside*). Have I done wisely in returning to life? Will they obey and respect me as before? May not some of the mysterious reverence which attaches to me—Bah! This is weakness! But I have heard of so many idols, private and public, relegated eventually to oblivion and neglect.

COUPLETS.—BUMBO.

(*Words by Frank Desprez.*)

When a fashionable tenor in a fascinating way,
Unutterably yearning, just evades his upper A;
Then ladies of all ages sit and simper, stare and sigh,
And adore his locks luxuriant and deep and rolling eye;
But as middle age approaches, and he takes to singing flat,
And is getting rather bald, and unromantically fat,
Then they transfer their devotion to some adolescent elf,
They have found another idol—*that* one's put upon the shelf.

When a trav'ller equatorial returns from foreign parts,
With a manner dictatorial, and photographs and charts,
They list in rapt attention to the tales he has to tell,
And they dine him, and they wine him, and they marry him as well.
Then come rumours, and ill-humours—tales of quite another kind,
As to comrades half-deserted, and contingents left behind;
And that traveller, indignant, writes and justifies himself,
But—well, they get another idol—*that* one's put upon the shelf.

BUMBO. Now, let my commands be obeyed, and leave me.

HYMN TO BUMBO.

PYJAMA, SUTTEE, CHEETAH, *and Male and Female Chorus*

Hail, Bumbo!
Bumbo the Mentor!
Guardian of the Sun, and of the Moon, and of the Twinkling Stars!
Curator of the Brooks, the Rivers, and the Rolling Seas!
Ruler of the Beasts, Custodian of the Birds, and Commander-in-chief
    of the Little Fishes!
Chief Librarian of the Book of Fate, and Responsible Managing
    Director of the Wheel of Fortune!
Hail, Bumbo, hail!

                        [Exeunt all but BUMBO.

BUMBO. I think I have done an excellent morning's work.

Enter CHINNA.

CHINNA (*aside*). Then it *is* true. The Idol has really come to life.
(*Looks at* BUMBO). He's not so very bad-looking. (*Then, with a
sudden shock*) Ah!

BUMBO (*aside*). What a nice little person! (*aloud*). Excuse
me—is anything the matter? May I?——

CHINNA (*aside, feeling her heart*). Is it? . . . Can it be? . . .
Impossible . . . And yet . . . the symptoms are all here. He's
not *at all* bad-looking—an idol—a deity. What am I to think?

BUMBO. What is your name, little one?

CHINNA. Chinna Loofa.

BUMBO. How sweet? Married?

CHINNA. Not as yet.

BUMBO. How fortunate! (*Takes her chin*).

CHINNA. Don't do that, please, sir.

BUMBO. Have no fear. Remember I am made of wood. I am
perfectly harmless, I assure you. How would you like to be an Idol's
bride, eh, pretty one?

CHINNA (*aside*). It's all right this time!

BUMBO. And sit on a shelf?

CHINNA. Oh, sir!

BUMBO. Would not the situation be novel?

CHINNA. Oh no, I've already been there eighteen months.

BUMBO, Where?

CHINNA (*sighing*). On the shelf.

BUMBO. Not on mine. (*Pause.*) Well, what do you say?

CHINNA (*aloud, throwing herself into his arms*). My heart has spoken. I am yours.

BUMBO (*aside*). Generous readiness! (*aloud*). By the bye, before we go any further, we had better understand each other clearly.

CHINNA (*on his breast—softly*). Settlements?

BUMBO. No.

CHINNA. Oh!

BUMBO. You are aware that marriage isn't what it was?

CHINNA. I am aware of the danger, nay, the positive wickedness, of incurring the bitterness of a baulked individuality; and, what's more, I don't intend to.

BUMBO. And of the necessity of self-development at any price?

CHINNA. And of the "absurdity of living with a strange man."

BUMBO (*starting suspiciously*). Eh, you don't mean me?

CHINNA. Well, you *are* a little peculiar.

BUMBO. It runs in the family.

CHINNA. Heredity?

BUMBO. Exactly. So you think we shall suit each other?

CHINNA. Down to the ground. Our views of matrimony are so rational.

BUMBO. Not to say revolutionary.

DUET & COMIC CARMAGNOLE.

(*Words by Frank Desprez.*)

BUMBO. I shall flirt and fandangle though people may talk,
BOTH.   Vive, vive la liberté!
BUMBO. Nor my idiosyncrasy banefully balk,
BOTH.   Vive, vive la liberté!
BUMBO. I shall find my affinities just where I please,
BOTH.   Vive, vive la liberté!
BUMBO. And if you object, I shall use Ibsenese!
    Vive, vive la liberté!
      Vive, vive,
        V'là ce qu'arrive,
      Vive, vive,
        La liberté!

CHINNA. I shall dance with whomever I like—barring *you,*
BOTH.   Vive, vive la liberté!
CHINNA. And have hangers-on, say a dozen or two,
BOTH.   Vive, vive la liberté!

CHINNA. I shall go out at eve, though your leave you begrudge,

BOTH.   Vive, vive la liberté !

CHINNA. And if you prevent me I'll speak to a Judge,

BOTH.   Vive, vive la liberté

             Vive, vive, &c.

BUMBO. But one thing occurs at this moment to me,

BOTH.   Vive, vive la liberté !

CHINNA. I think I can guess it—your meaning I see—

BOTH.   Vive, vive la liberté

BUMBO. If the fetters of wedlock so lightly enthrall—

BOTH.   Vive, vive la liberté !

CHINNA. Is it really worth while to get married at all ?

BOTH.   Vive, vive la liberté !

BUMBO.   Vive, vive,

CHINNA. French, I believe—ah !

BOTH.   Vive, vive,
             La liberté !

BUMBO. Permit me. (*Offers his arm; they turn and meet* PUNKA, *who enters from back, wearing an outcast's dress.*) You are prepared for your doom, I see.

PUNKA. Yes ; excuse me, there's a blue-bottle just on the tip of your——(*pats fly on his nose*).

BUMBO (*pushing him away*). Don't maul me about ! Wherever you touch you leave a finger-mark, and I don't like it.

PUNKA. And would you, in cold blood, condemn my son and myself to a horrible death ?

BUMBO. My only regret is that there are not more of you. If you had a lot of relatives, this would have been the happiest day of my life. (*Moves away with* CHINNA.)

PUNKA (*aside, breathing heavily, as though wrestling with his conscience*). Yes, yes, yes ! Like a worm, you may tread upon a phrenological bump until it turns. (*To* BUMBO, *eagerly*) I *have* some relations—cousins—hundreds of them !

BUMBO. Good ! We'll have a glorious execution this afternoon. I condemn them *all* to death !

CHINNA (*alarmed*). All !

BUMBO. All !

PUNKA. Including the half cousins, the quarters, and the fractions?

BUMBO. Yes.

PUNKA (*aside, gloating*). Ha, ha, ha! Pyjama is one of the fractions. I look forward to the ceremony with a degree of gratification that is absolutely diabolical.

ing this last speech CHINNA *is seen to converse with* BUMBO *aside, and obtain from him an assurance that she will be exempt from the sentence*).

TRIO.—BUMBO, PUNKA, CHINNA.

PUNKA.   You will sign our death-warrant to-day?
BUMBO.   Of course.
CHINNA (*aside*).   But you won't include *my* name, I pray?
BUMBO (*aside*).   Of course.
PUNKA.   And ere set of sun
                The deed will be done,
                In the regular orthodox way?
BUMBO.   Of course.
PUNKA.   You'll indict us all in the decree?
BUMBO.   Of course.
CHINNA (*aside*).   But you'll make an exception of me?
BUMBO (*aside*).   Of course.
PUNKA.   You say you'll prefer,
                The homicide per

C R O C O D I L E

BUMBO.   Of course.
PUNKA.   C
BUMBO.   R
CHINNA.   O
PUNKA.   C
BUMBO.   O
CHINNA.   D
PUNKA.   I
BUMBO.   L
CHINNA.   E
PUNKA.   In agony I will cheerfully die
                If locked in a cousin's caress,
           And that is the why and the what and the wherefore,
                The when and the nevertheless.
ALL.   Yes, that is, &c. (*Dance.*)

PUNKA. You will chain us all up in a row?

BUMBO. Of course.

CHINNA (*aside*). With a single exception, you know.

BUMBO (*aside*). Of course.

PUNKA.
And then with a grin,
You'll push us all in,
To the crocodiles waiting below?

BUMBO. Of course, to the crocodiles, &c.

PUNKA. You will watch our death-struggles with glee?

BUMBO. Of course.

CHINNA (*aside*). But you won't get the least glimpse of me.

BUMBO. Of course.

PUNKA.
'Twill make a rare stir,
This massacre per

C R O C O D I L E

BUMBO. Of course.

PUNKA. C

BUMBO. R

CHINNA. O

PUNKA. C

BUMBO. O

CHINNA. D

PUNKA. I

BUMBO. L

CHINNA. E

I'll lie in the jaw of an al-li-ga-*tor*,
And smile at my cousins' distress,
And that is the why and the what and the wherefore,
The when and the nevertheless.

[*Exeunt, dancing.*

Enter BEEBEE, *timorously, at back.*

BEEBEE. At last I am back at the old spot. I shall never forget that dreadful moment after we sailed, when I discovered that Indru was not on board, and that every breath of wind bore me farther from him. Where can he be?

Enter at back INDRU, *disguised.*

INDRU. I am trapped ! The city gates are guarded, and even in this disguise my features would be recognized. (*Sees* BEEBEE) Beebee !

BEEBEE. Indru ! (*they embrace*).

INDRU. But where is Currie, and all the girls ?

BEEBEE. Currie is here, but nearly all the girls have accepted other engagements in Europe.

INDRU. What a pity ! But my Beebee has been true to me— she has returned !

BEEBEE. Yes.

INDRU. You have brought no one's heart away ?

BEEBEE. I have brought nothing but this gem. (*Indicating pendant at her neck.*)

INDRU. What a brilliant stone ! How curiously it is cut !

BEEBEE. It was said to be a charm that would give good fortune to her who carried it.

INDRU. Alas, Beebee ! It has not bestowed it yet.

SONG.—INDRU.

When all the world was bright, love,
    And every night was day,
And all our thoughts were light, love,
    And all our work was play,
We smiled, and smiled again, love,
    At others' hapless lot,
We thought there was no pain, love,
    Because we felt it not.

BOTH.
            The earth was green, and blue the sea,
            The world was bright to you and me.

Now all the world is dark, love,
    And every day is night,
And dying is the spark, love,
    That once was burning bright.
The sun will never more, love,
    Rise from his golden bed,
To light us as of yore, love,
    For all the world is dead.

BOTH.
            The earth is bare, and black the sea,
            The world is dead to you and me.

Enter PUNKA, *guarded, with large scroll.*

PUNKA. I can't find Pyjama. (*Seeing* INDRU.) You still here, and—what—Beebee! (*To* BEEBEE.) Have you returned to contemplate the misery you have caused?

BEEBEE. No, great Rajah.

PUNKA. Don't address me as Rajah.

BEEBEE. Why not?

PUNKA. Well, I'd Rajah you didn't! I and Indru are both condemned. Pyjama's Rajah now.

BEEBEE. Is there no hope of escape?

PUNKA. None whatever. Besides, I am now really resigned to my fate. I don't think I want to escape. Look at that! (*Unfolds scroll.*) Such an exquisite joke of mine!

INDRU. What is it?

PUNKA. A complete list of my relatives, three-hundred-and-seventy-four all told. I have persuaded the far-seeing Bumbo to extend his sentence to the cousins. He doesn't know that his new Rajah, Pyjama, is one of them. Ha! ha! ha!

BEEBEE. But if you could escape, you would still have the gratification of knowing that they were dead.

PUNKA. But I shouldn't have the gratification of seeing them die. I wouldn't miss the sight for anything. The pleasure won't last long, I know; but it will be delicious while it's on.

INDRU. Would you sacrifice your life for the sake of a joke?

PUNKA. I'm not sure that I wouldn't. It's the first joke I've ever made, and I think a lot of it. The ornamental water is now being baited with penny buns and other appetizing crocodilic *hors-d'œuvres*, and by three o'clock it will literally swarm with the sacred saurians, at which hour the whole three-hundred-and-seventy-four of us will be chained together, myself at one end and Pyjama at the other. Bumbo has kindly promised to personally conduct the funeral service, which will be musical throughout; and at a given signal the whole string of us will be pitched into the water—Pyjama's end goes in first. Ha! ha! ha!

(CURRIE, BANYAN, KALEE, *and* TIFFIN *have come on listening.*)

BEEBEE. Your Majesty must not sacrifice your valuable life to an exaggerated sense of humour. Ah! there is Currie—he will help us! (*to* CURRIE). Do let us try and get to Europe again, and smuggle these two off with us!

CURRIE. Now what is the good of asking me to do that? I can't go to Europe without a troupe. Where's my troupe? Gone! Scattered! All my prettiest girls have deserted me!

INDRU. Not the prettiest! They have returned.

BANYAN. I quite agree with you.

TIFFIN. So do I.

KALEE. And so do I.

BANYAN. There are three of us left, and not the least talented.

TIFFIN. Nor the least beautiful.

CURRIE. What's the use of three? You can't have a allet of three—you can't even have a front row of three—and the public know so much nowadays, I don't think they'd even stand a quartette of three.

PUNKA. If you take us two, you can have a quartette of five. (*indicating* INDRU, *himself, and the three girls.*) That ought to settle them!

CURRIE. Nonsense! What could you do? They've got enough ex-monarchs in Europe already—you wouldn't draw!

INDRU. Why shouldn't we dance?

CURRIE. Because you don't know how.

BEEBEE. Oh, Indru dances exceedingly well. I've given him several lessons already.

PUNKA. Oh, I can dance. Look here!

CURRIE. You'll have to learn a great deal more than that. If we get back to Europe I shall introduce a novelty. The second part of our entertainment will consist of the dances of each country we visit, given by Baboo Currie's celebrated Nautch Troupe. There's a sensation for you!

SONG *and* DANCE.—Currie *and Others.*

(Words by Frank Desprez.)

CURRIE. If we travel by way of Brindisi,
 Cross the Continent, get to Berlin,
We must do and must dance—just as we see
 The folk of the country we're in.
In the valse with its airy attraction
 We'll affect to find infinite bliss,
And drive Deutschers straight to distraction
 By elegant actions like this—

 (Dances valse as he sings refrain.)

 Round, round, ever around,
 Toes just touching the ground,
 Head bent, languishing*lee*—
 That's how they do it in Germanee!

ALL.   Round, round, &c.
       (They dance.)

When halting at giddy Gibraltar,
 Or stopping at sunny Cadiz,
Your style will immediately alter,
 Turn your toes and attention to this—
    (Strikes cachuca attitude.)
To boleros your mind you'll abandon,
 And without any trouble or fuss,
The light castanet lay your hand on,
 And conduct yourself cleverly thus—*(Does cachuca.)*
 Slide, slide, recede and advance,
 Flirt fan, prettily prance, *(kneels)*
 Swing arms—again and again,
 That's how they do it in sunny Spain.

In London a little while stopt,
 In the mad metropolitan maze,
With alacrity then you'll adopt
 The latest society craze.
To don the " accordion pleat "
 Does every young lady prepare,
And does wonderful things with her feet,
 Though old-fashioned people may stare.

(He mimics skirt dancer à la Guards' Burlesque)

 Arms high, skirts lifted *so,*
 Head back, well-pointed toe,
 Neat hose, attitude free,
 That's how they do in Societee ! *(Dance.)*

(CURRIE *and* INDRU *exit dancing, each taking two girls.* PUNKA
follows last. Enter PYJAMA *in Rajah's robes, with attendants.*)

PYJAMA (*seeing* PUNKA). Stop, fellow!

PUNKA. Oh, I was looking for you—I wanted to show you——

PYJAMA. What is it?

PUNKA (*handing up scroll*). Read!

PYJAMA. What's this? (*Collapses.*)

PUNKA. Too bad of Bumbo, isn't it? (*Chuckles.*) I haven't
told the others yet. I thought I'd bring you the good news first.
Don't give up, old chap! Be brave! Think what a nice family
party we shall make, and what fun there'll be.

PYJAMA. Fun? There'll be no fun.

PUNKA. Oh, yes, there will—for the crocodiles.

PYJAMA. Don't!

PUNKA. I've arranged for a photographer to take us in a family
group before we are pitched into the water, and no expense will be
spared to make the function a huge success.

PYJAMA. Stay! I am not your cousin!

PUNKA. What?

PYJAMA. I merely claimed a relationship to obtain a post at
Court.

PUNKA. Good Heavens! And the others?

PYJAMA. Just the same—they're not your cousins, either.

PUNKA (*upset*). Then I suppose you'll none of you be included
in the execution?

PYJAMA. No; but we'll all come and look on. You'd better
get ready.

PUNKA. Oh, I'm in no great hurry. I'll tell them to discharge
the orchestra. (*Going.*)

PYJAMA. No such thing. Bumbo decreed that you should die in
half an hour; there's only ten minutes left. Await me at the Palace
gates. (*To* PUNKA.) There'll be lots of fun for the crocodiles, eh?

PUNKA (*aside*). I don't think so much of that joke, after all.

[*Exit* PUNKA.

(*Enter at back*, CURRIE *looking anxiously about.*)

CURRIE. Where's Punka got to? (*Sees* PYJAMA.) Your Ex——
I mean your Highness. (*Salaams.*)

PYJAMA. What, Currie—back again! The proprietor of the
cleverest Nautch troupe in Hindustan.

CURRIE (*with ineffable conceit*). Your Highness—the *only* Nautch
troupe in the *world*.

PYJAMA. Haven't I always said so? (BEEBEE, BANYAN, KALEE, *and* TIFFIN *enter quietly at back, and listen.*) Wasn't I always one of your best patrons?

CURRIE. Ye—yes. (*Aside*) He always came with an order.

PYJAMA (*seeing* BEEBEE). What, Beebee too! Fascinating little Beebee! This is splendid. (*Rubbing his hands.*) We'll have such an entertainment in the grounds this evening. "Under the immediate patronage of His Highness Pyjama, Rajah of Chutneypore"— my name in large capitals, you know.

CURRIE. How can I express———

PYJAMA. Don't! There is nothing I adore so much as one of those vocal dances of yours. (*To* BEEBEE) Oh, you little Terpsichorean chick-a-biddy!

BEEBEE (*aside to* CURRIE). A last chance! We might keep Pyjama here and make him miss the hour of the execution. That headstrong Idol may then turn his anger against Pyjama and forget his prey.

BANYAN (*to* PYJAMA). You haven't seen me dance!

KALEE. You haven't heard *me* sing!

TIFFIN. I've improved wonderfully since I've been away.

ALL THREE. Like to see our notices? (*producing simultaneously newspaper cuttings*).

PYJAMA. Their notices! The darlings!

BEEBEE (*coming down and roguishly confronting him*). *Would* you like to hear my latest song and dance?

PYJAMA. Dee-licious idea! (*To* CURRIE) Let them begin at once!

CURRIE. Certainly, your Majesty! Girls, take your places!

(*During* Symphony CURRIE *places seat for* PYJAMA, *gives him programme, refuses, scandalized, to take a fee, and hands him operaglasses. Courtiers and Poor Relations enter.*)

VOCAL NAUTCH DANCE.—BEEBEE, CURRIE, BANYAN, KALEE, TIFFIN, CHORUS.

BEEBEE.	Gently bear my lady to her chamber,
OTHERS.	Cubbadar!
BEEBEE.	Lay her softly on her silken bed;
OTHERS.	Cubbadar!
BEEBEE.	Lightly spread her tresses o'er the pillow,
OTHERS.	Cubbadar!

BEEBEE.	Draw the curtains close about her head.
OTHERS.	Cubbadar!
BEEBEE.	Quickly close the window o'er the river,
OTHERS.	Cubbadar!
BEEBEE.	Lock the door, and quench the flaring light.
OTHERS.	Cubbadar!
BEEBEE.	Buzzing comes the plundering mosquito,
OTHERS.	Cubbadar!
BEEBEE.	Like a brawling bandit of the night.
OTHERS.	Cubbadar!
BEEBEE.	Hark! he comes!
OTHERS.	Uzz!
BEEBEE.	How he hums!
OTHERS.	Uzz!
BEEBEE.	Nearer, nearer, nearer he approaches,
	Through the darkness, like an Evil One;
	Closer, closer, closer he encroaches;
	Whisper! he is pausing! Hush! he's gone!

(The others give a buzzing accompaniment to these last four lines, in imitation of a mosquito.)

BEEBEE.	Tenderly allay my lady's terror,
OTHERS.	Cubbadar!
BEEBEE.	Close her eyes and bid her sink to rest.
OTHERS.	Cubbadar!
BEEBEE.	Gently rock her into peaceful slumber,
OTHERS.	Cubbadar!
BEEBEE.	Chant the lullaby she loves the best.
OTHERS.	Cubbadar!
BEEBEE.	Silent now is all the sleeping city,
OTHERS.	Cubbadar!
BEEBEE.	Save the splash upon the distant shore.
OTHERS.	Cubbadar!
BEEBEE.	Listen! Once again comes the mosquito!
OTHERS.	Cubbadar!
BEEBEE.	Buzzing at my lady's chamber door.
OTHERS.	Cubbadar!
BEEBEE.	Hark! he comes, &c.

(After dance, thunder and lightning. Enter BUMBO, *with* CHINNA *on his arm, followed by Attendants.* CURRIE *and the Girls go up.)*

BUMBO. I am disappointed in you, Pyjama! For twenty minutes I have been waiting the arrival of that pleasant tickling sensation, and I have awaited in vain. (*Sternly*). Produce the prisoners!

(PUNKA *and* INDRU *enter in charge of guards.*)

PUNKA. One moment — excuse me — I have an important communication to make. (*Advancing to* BUMBO, *pointing to his eye, and speaking with great warmth.*) Behind that green shade is a cavity.

BUMBO (*furious and threatening*). Ah!

PUNKA. In that cavity there once reposed a diamond. (BUMBO, *enraged, lifts his hand.*) That diamond was one dark night abstracted. (BUMBO *buries his face in his hands.*) The thief was—*Pyjama!*

(BUMBO, *speechless, turns to* PYJAMA, *who trembles and collapses as* BUMBO *strides towards him.* BUMBO *motions Priests, who seize* PYJAMA *and take him off.*)

PUNKA (*aside*). At last! It's a long joke that has no turning!

BUMBO. Away with them!

CHINNA (*appealing to* BUMBO). Spare them for *my* sake!

BEEBEE. And for mine! (*She and* CHINNA *get one on each side of him.* BUMBO *is obviously amenable to the charms of female beauty, and turning to* BEEBEE.)

BUMBO. What a pretty face! (*Chucks her chin; annoyance of* CHINNA, *who pulls him away.*) Very sorry, but I could not disappoint the dear crocodiles. (*Violently*). Take them away! (*Playfully to* BEEBEE). Bye, bye! (*Starts, with his eye riveted on the pendant at her neck.*) Ha!

CHINNA. What is the matter, dear?

BUMBO. It is—my left eye! Do you see?

CHINNA. Where?

BUMBO. My left eye suspended round that sweet little creature's neck! Come to my arms, my long lost eye! (*Embraces* BEEBEE; CHINNA *pulls him away; turning to* BEEBEE *again.*) But how did you come by that jewel?

BEEBEE. It was left at the stage door.

BUMBO. Anonymous, I presume?

BEEBEE (*indignant*). Anonymous, of course. I should not have received it otherwise. (*General incredulity.*) But he called the next day. (*General relief.*)

INDRU (*angrily, stepping forward*). Ah!

BEEBEE. Then I told him I could not love him, and he must take the diamond back; but he wouldn't, and said I must keep it, and it would bring me luck.

BUMBO. And so it shall! You have, my girl, removed my greatest sorrow, and in return I will grant you any request you like to make.

BEEBEE. Let Punka and Indru be acquitted and restored to their rank!

BUMBO. Hum! Well, I suppose I must. (PUNKA *is released,* INDRU *comes forward and throws off his disguise.*)

PUNKA. My dear Bumbo, you're a brick! (*slapping him on back*).

BUMBO. I'm not a brick, I'm a wooden idol, and if you strike me on the back again, I shall retaliate in a manner that you will not enjoy. (*Addressing the diamond*) You beauty! (*kisses it*) I thought I should never see you or see with you again! Bless you! (*To those near him*) Pardon me! (*Removes the shade from his eye, appears to press the diamond into its place, and then looks about with eyes wide open.*) How's that?

PUNKA. Not out!

INDRU. Charming!

PUNKA. Suits you admirably!

BUMBO. Yes, I think it does. Upon my word, it makes me feel fifteen hundred years younger! (*Struts. Then to* CHINNA.) You are still willing to be an Idol's bride?

CHINNA (*nodding*). Anybody's bride will do.

BUMBO. And to be turned into wood, and sit always by my side? (CHINNA *assents.*) Fetch the throne. Bless you, my children! And now for a roar of cannon, a crash of bells, and a blare of trumpets, and Bumbo will return to his shelf for ever!

FINALE.

BUMBO.	And this is the Idol, grave and staid,
CHINNA.	That wooed and won the simple maid,
BANYAN.	That came to be of Punka's train
TIFFIN.	By means of the ingenious brain
INDRU.	That sent my Beebee o'er the main
BEEBEE.	To where I practised once again
CURRIE.	The dainty step her teacher taught, Which from her fond admirer bought
KALEE.	The wondrous, rare, and precious stone

BUMBO.	That saved my eyesight,
PUNKA.	And the throne
	Of the Rajah of Chutneypore ;
INDRU.	For long may my father in happiness reign.
ALL.	Vive, vive, sa Majesté !
CHINNA.	And long may my Bumbo my Idol remain !
ALL.	Vive, vive la liberté !
BEEBEE (to INDRU).	And ne'er may your heart from your Beebee remove,
ALL.	Vive, vive la liberté.
PUNKA.	And long may the public my edicts approve.
ALL.	Vive, vive sa Majesté !
	Vive, vive tout ce qu'arrive,
	Vive, Vive sa Majesté !

Sedan chair brought on. BUMBO *and* CHINNA *take their places in it, and make angular and eccentric motions indicative of turning to wood. The Priests take them up, and are carrying them off to the temple at the descent of the*

CURTAIN.

HENDERSON & SPALDING, Printers, 3 and 5, Marylebone Lane, London, W.

IVANHOE
Grand Romantic Opera.

ADAPTED FROM SIR WALTER SCOTT'S NOVEL BY
JULIAN STURGIS.

THE MUSIC BY
ARTHUR SULLIVAN.

Now being Performed at the Royal English Opera House with Immense Success

	s.	D.
VOCAL SCORE (arranged by Ernest Ford) ... net	7	6
" (Bound) ... ... "	10	0
PIANOFORTE SOLO (arranged by Ernest Ford) ... "	4	0
LIBRETTO ... ... "	1	0

VOCAL MUSIC.

The King's Song, "I ask nor wealth, nor courtier's praise" (for Bass)	4	0
Ivanhoe's Song, "Come, gentle sleep" (for Tenor) ...	4	0
The Friar's Song, "Ho, jolly Jenkin" (for Bass) ...	4	0
Sir Brian's Song, "Woo thou thy snowflake" (for Baritone)	4	0
Duet—Rowena and Ivanhoe, "How oft beneath the far-off Syrian skies" (Soprano and Tenor)... ...	4	0
Rebecca's Recit. and Prayer, "Lord of our chosen race" (Soprano)	4	0

PIANOFORTE ARRANGEMENTS.

GODFREY'S SELECTION, as played by all Military Bands (Solo)	4	0
Do. do. (Duet)	5	0
KUHE'S FANTASIA	4	0
BOYTON SMITH'S FANTASIA...	4	0
SMALLWOOD'S FANTASIA	4	0

VIOLIN AND PIANOFORTE.

BERTHOLD TOURS' SELECTION	5	0
GODFREY'S SELECTION for Orchestra, full Band net	3	4
" " Octuor ... ... "	2	8
" " for full Military Band ... "	15	0
TERRY'S SELECTION for Violin Solo ... ... "	1	6

LONDON:

THE NAUTCH GIRL

Or, THE RAJAH OF CHUTNEYPORE.

A New Indian Comic Opera.

WRITTEN BY   MUSIC BY

GEORGE DANCE & FRANK DESPREZ.   EDWARD SOLOMON.

	s.	D.
VOCAL SCORE	5	0
Ditto bound	7	6
PIANOFORTE ARRANGEMENT	3	0
LIBRETTO	1	0

VOCAL MUSIC.

	s.	D.
"The sun was setting." Sung by Mr. Courtice Pounds ...	4	0
"When our shackles are undone." Duet. Sung by Miss Lenore Snyder and Mr. Courtice Pounds	4	0
"And this is the royal diadem." Sung by Mr. Rutland Barrington	4	0
"Do not think me overbold." Sung by Miss Jessie Bond	4	0
"Vive, vive la liberté." Duet and Comic Carmagnole. Sung by Miss Jessie Bond and Mr. Denny...	4	0
"From her hive the bee." Sung by Miss Lenore Snyder	4	0
"When all the world was bright." Sung by Mr. Courtice Pounds	4	0

DANCE MUSIC.

		s.	D.
Quadrille	P. Bucalossi	4	0
Lancers	P. Bucalossi	4	0
Waltz	P. Bucalossi	4	0

PIANOFORTE ARRANGEMENTS.

		s.	D.
Godfrey's Selection, as played by all the Military Bands. Solo		4	0
Ditto ditto	Duet	5	0
Smallwood's Fantasia		4	0
Kuhe's Fantasia		4	0

VIOLIN AND PIANOFORTE.

	s.	D.
Tours' Selection	5	0

	s.	D.
Godfrey's Selection for Military Band	15	0
Ditto for Full Orchestra	3	4
Ditto for Octuor	2	8
Terry's Selection for Violin Solo	1	6